TONY BLAIR

A Real-Life Reader Biography

Wayne Wilson and Jim Whiting

Mitchell Lane Publishers, Inc.

P.O. Box 619 • Bear, Delaware 19701
www.mitchelllane.com

Printing   1   2   3   4   5   6   7   8   9   10

Real-Life Reader Biographies

Paula Abdul	Christina Aguilera	Marc Anthony	Lance Armstrong
Drew Barrymore	**Tony Blair**	Brandy	Garth Brooks
Kobe Bryant	Sandra Bullock	Mariah Carey	Aaron Carter
Cesar Chavez	Roberto Clemente	Christopher Paul Curtis	Roald Dahl
Oscar De La Hoya	Trent Dimas	Celine Dion	Sheila E.
Gloria Estefan	Mary Joe Fernandez	Michael J. Fox	Andres Galarraga
Sarah Michelle Gellar	Jeff Gordon	Virginia Hamilton	Mia Hamm
Melissa Joan Hart	Salma Hayek	Jennifer Love Hewitt	Faith Hill
Hollywood Hogan	Katie Holmes	Enrique Iglesias	Allen Iverson
Janet Jackson	Derek Jeter	Steve Jobs	Alicia Keys
Michelle Kwan	Bruce Lee	Jennifer Lopez	Cheech Marin
Ricky Martin	Mark McGwire	Alyssa Milano	Mandy Moore
Chuck Norris	Tommy Nuñez	Rosie O'Donnell	Mary-Kate and Ashley Olsen
Rafael Palmeiro	Gary Paulsen	Colin Powell	Freddie Prinze, Jr.
Condoleezza Rice	Julia Roberts	Robert Rodriguez	J.K. Rowling
Keri Russell	Winona Ryder	Cristina Saralegui	Charles Schulz
Arnold Schwarzenegger	Selena	Maurice Sendak	Dr. Seuss
Shakira	Alicia Silverstone	Jessica Simpson	Sinbad
Jimmy Smits	Sammy Sosa	Britney Spears	Julia Stiles
Ben Stiller	Sheryl Swoopes	Shania Twain	Liv Tyler
Robin Williams	Vanessa Williams	Venus Williams	Tiger Woods

Library of Congress Cataloging-in-Publication Data
Wilson, Wayne, 1953-
     Tony Blair/Wayne Wilson.
          p. cm.—(A real-life reader biography)
     Includes index.
     Summary: Profiles the popular Labour party member who, in 1997 at the age of forty-four, became Britain's youngest prime minister in over two hundred years, and details his support of the war against terrorism begun in 2001.
     ISBN 1-58415-143-9 (lib bdg.)
     1. Blair, Tony, 1953—Juvenile literature. 2. Prime ministers—Great Britain—Biography—Juvenile literature. [1. Blair, Tony, 1953- 2. Prime ministers.] I. Title. II. Series.
DA591.B56 W55 2003
941.085'9—dc21
                                                                                                                                  2002022139

ABOUT THE AUTHOR: Wayne Wilson was born and raised in Los Angeles. He received a Master of Arts in Education from the University of California, Los Angeles. For 16 years he was co-owner and president of a pioneering and innovative publishing company specializing in multicultural designs. Recently, he completed interviews with influential Latino men throughout the country and wrote over 160 biographies. He lives in Venice Beach, CA with his wife and daughter. **Jim Whiting** has been a journalist, writer, editor, and photographer for more than 20 years. In addition to a lengthy stint as publisher of *Northwest Runner* magazine, Mr. Whiting has contributed to the *Seattle Times*, *Conde Nast Traveler*, *Newsday*, and *Saturday Evening Post*. He has edited more than 20 titles in the Mitchell Lane Real-Life Reader Biography series and Unlocking the Secrets of Science. He lives in Washington state with his wife and two teenage sons.

PHOTO CREDITS: cover: Reuters/Ian Hodgson/Corbis; p. 4 Globe Photos; p. 6 Corbis; p. 9 AP Photo/Susan Walsh; pp. 12, 15, 19, 22, 24, 27 Globe Photos; p. 30 Reuters/Russell Boyce/Corbis

Table of Contents

Chapter 1   The United States' Best Friend 5

Chapter 2   The Young Rebel 11

Chapter 3   Rock Bands and College Life 17

Chapter 4   From Lawyer to Leader................. 21

Chapter 5   Family Life in the Spotlight 26

Chapter 6   What the Future May Hold 29

Chronology 32

Index 32

Chapter 1
The United States' Best Friend

On the afternoon of September 11, 2001, British Prime Minister Tony Blair was in a hotel room in the seaside resort town of Brighton, England. He was working on a controversial speech that he was scheduled to deliver that evening to the Trades Union Congress, a group that represents most of the organized workers in England.

Suddenly he received the horrifying news that the World Trade Center in New York City had been attacked by suicide terrorists who hijacked commercial airliners and deliberately flew them into the twin thousand-foot-high towers. Thousands of people died when roaring fires engulfed the buildings and soon caused them to collapse. Most of the victims

The World Trade Center had been attacked by suicide terrorists.

were Americans but some were from other countries including England.

He immediately scrapped the

Tony Blair meets with soldiers in Afghanistan.

speech that he was working on and began to write one that was entirely different.

That evening, in a voice trembling with emotion, Blair told his audience, "It is hard even to contemplate the utter carnage and terror which has engulfed so many innocent people. This mass terrorism is the new evil in our world.

"The people who perpetrate it have no regard whatever for the sanctity or value of human life. This is not a battle between the United States of America and terrorism but between the free and democratic world and terrorism.

"We therefore here in Britain stand shoulder to shoulder with our American friends in this hour of tragedy and we, like them, will not rest until this evil is driven from our world."

From the moment he made that statement, Blair proved that he was as good as his word. It quickly became apparent that Osama bin Laden, a former Saudi Arabian prince, was behind the attack. He had used Afghanistan as his base of operations with the approval of the Taliban, the group that formed the government of the country.

So Blair committed thousands of British troops and other elements of its armed forces, including airplanes and warships, to help the U.S. in its attack against the Taliban and Osama bin Laden.

He also traveled throughout the world, logging thousands of miles to help put together an international coalition to assist in the campaign against the Taliban regime and the terrorist forces it allowed to operate inside its borders.

He covered about one country every two days, meeting with presidents, prime ministers, sultans and sheiks, chancellors and emirs. Because the attackers claimed to be acting in the name of the religion of Islam,

Blair committed thousands of British troops to help the U.S. in its attack against the Taliban.

Blair began reading the Quran—the holy book of Islam. He wanted to gain a greater idea of how the Islamic world thinks.

He also studied volumes of material about Afghanistan. He wrote newspaper and magazine columns and spoke to angry leaders in the Arab and Islamic worlds explaining the U.S. and British bombing of Afghanistan.

He did all this knowing that it could be personally dangerous. A TV interviewer in Oman, an oil-rich Islamic country on the Arabian Sea, asked Blair if he was worried about his life being endangered. A radical Islamic group had proclaimed that he was a "legitimate target."

But his response was, "No, I'm afraid it comes with the job."

This wasn't the first time that Blair had taken a leading role in international politics since becoming prime minister in 1997 at the age of 44. That made him the youngest English prime minister since Lord Liverpool in 1812.

Early in 1999, the 19 countries of the North Atlantic Treaty Organization, or NATO as it is commonly known, began a bombing campaign to remove Slobodan Milosevic's Serbian army and police from the disputed territory of Kosovo. Visiting nearby Macedonia, Blair saw

At the age of 44, Blair was the youngest prime minister since 1812.

a region filled with refugees. Almost all of them were Muslims, or believers in Islam. He said, "I felt an anger so strong, a loathing of what Milosevic stands for so powerful, that I pledged to those refugees, as I pledge to you now, that Milosevic and his hideous racial genocide will be defeated. To walk away would be a breach of faith to thousands of innocent civilians."

Thereafter, the prime minister almost single-handedly got NATO to change its los-

Tony Blair met with U. S. President George W. Bush after the terrorist attacks on September 11, 2001.

Blair convinced NATO to change its tactics in the Kosovo air war.

ing tactics in the Kosovo air war. He convinced a reluctant U.S. President Bill Clinton and other NATO leaders that the war could not be confined to high altitude bombing in Kosovo. It had to be carried to the Serbian capitol of Belgrade itself.

Weeks later Slobodan Milosevic surrendered. The war in Kosovo, Blair stated, was "a just war, based not on any territorial ambitions but on values."

Chapter 2
The Young Rebel

Anthony Charles Lynton Blair was born in Edinburgh, Scotland on May 6, 1953. He joined his brother William, who had been born three years earlier. The family would welcome the birth of Sarah in 1956.

Tony's father, Leo Charles Lynton Blair, was the son of two actors and dancers, Charles Parsons (whose stage name was Jimmy Lynton) and Celia Ridgeway. Because they weren't married when Leo was born in 1923, the little boy was adopted by a couple who lived in Glasgow, Scotland named James and Mary Blair. James worked as a shipyard worker and the family didn't have much money.

Tony and his brother attended Durham Choristers School.

As a result, young Leo wasn't very well-educated while he was growing up. But he was determined to be successful. After his military service in World War II he studied law and eventually became a successful lawyer.

Tony's mother, Hazel Elizabeth Rosaleen Corscaden, was a housewife who was descended from a farming family in Northern Ireland. She was the stepdaughter of a butcher.

Tony in a class photograph

Soon after Tony's birth, the family moved back to Glasgow, where Leo had been raised, then spent three years in Adelaide, Australia. The family moved back to England in the late 1950s and settled in Durham, an industrial city about 50 miles south of the Scottish border, where Leo Blair taught law at Durham University. The Blair children grew up there. The boys attended Durham Choristers School, where they had to wear baggy shorts and striped ties. Because William was several grades ahead of him, Tony was nicknamed "Blair Two."

In 1963, when Tony was 10, Leo Blair ran for Parliament, which is very similar to the U.S. House of Representatives. But even though he was only 40, he suffered a stroke during the campaign and lost the ability to speak for three years. About this time, Sarah was hospitalized for two years with a juvenile form of rheumatoid arthritis. These setbacks caused the family severe financial and emotional distress.

Leo Blair passed his political ambitions on to his son. In what might have been a sign of things to come, Tony won a mock political election among his fellow students at Durham Choristers when he was 12.

His win didn't surprise many people. By that time, he was one of the best-known boys in the school with a reputation as a star athlete. And he was bright enough to skip a grade and still finish with the third-highest grades in his class.

He showed other qualities that were important for a future politician as well. Canon John Grove, the headmaster at Durham Choristers when Tony was there, remembered, "He was outgoing. If you needed a volunteer, he was the boy who always had his hand up."

Tony won a mock political election when he was 12 years old.

Tony Blair had another nickname. Many people called him the "smiling boy" because he always seemed to have a grin on his face.

"Tony had an almost impish smile, it could light up a room," Canon Grove added. "And when I see him on the television, I see that it has not gone."

In 1966, when he was 13, Tony graduated from Durham Choristers and enrolled in Fettes College in Edinburgh, which had become one of the most famous schools in Scotland after opening its doors in 1870. But even though it is called a college, Fettes is actually a combination of an elementary school and a high school.

Because Edinburgh is more than 100 miles away from Durham, Tony had to leave home and become a boarding student.

Although Tony had been a model pupil when he was at Durham Choristers, the harsh discipline at Fettes made him unhappy. According to one story, he ran away from the school and tried to stow away in an airplane. But he eventually made an adjustment to the different life that he led there. He participated in sports such as basketball, rugby, and cricket, which is similar to baseball. He played major parts in plays that Fettes students produced and received a great deal of praise for his performances.

He also acquired a reputation for being a rebel. He grew his hair long, greased it down with butter so that it would fit inside his collar, and often questioned the rules and regulations of the school.

Tony (left) questioned the rules of the school.

Eric Anderson, one of his housemasters, remembers that "I got used to that knock at my study door, followed by the grinning Blair face and a 15-minute argument about ways of doing things which the school ought to, he thought, change at once.

"Tony was full of life, maddening at times, full of himself and very argumentative. He was an expert at testing the rules to the limit, and I wouldn't swear that he stuck rigidly to the school rules on not drinking, smoking or breaking bounds. But he was a live wire and fun to have around."

And Nick Ryden, who became his friend at Fettes and would become his youngest son's godfather many years later, said, "Being a rebel would mean going down town without permission or questioning why you had to play sport on a Wednesday afternoon. I did go out to clubs a couple of times with Tony, where we would have to get through fences under the cover of darkness."

But a different housemaster at the school said that the teenager was "infuriating" and "the most difficult boy I ever had to deal with." Tony was paddled several times and came very close to being expelled a few weeks before he graduated.

Chapter 3
Rock Bands and College Life

After he graduated from Fettes in 1971, Blair took a year off and lived in London, where he worked as a bartender and on a construction site. He also managed a rock band and had plans to make it famous.

A picture taken during that time shows Blair and a friend perched on top of a van that they bought for less than $200. The young man who in 25 years would become the British leader has hair parted in the middle that falls onto his shoulders, his shirt is unbuttoned down to his waist, and he is barefoot. But he was different from many other members of what was then called the "counterculture." He kept a Bible next to his bed and didn't use drugs.

Tony kept a Bible next to his bed and did not use drugs.

In 1972 he entered the all-male St. John's College at Oxford University, which is near London and more than 100 miles from Durham. Because of his father's influence, he decided to study law. But his hair was even longer than it had been at Fettes and he often wore bizarre clothing. One day his father arrived to pick him up and didn't even recognize his son until Tony said, "Hi, Dad."

He soon became the lead singer and occasional guitar player for a rock band that was known as Ugly Rumours. One of the band members remembers that Blair would appear on stage trying to look like Mick Jagger of the Rolling Stones, wagging his finger and punching the air.

But in addition to his interest in rock music, he began to develop a serious side. He frequently engaged in conversations with his fellow students. One of them was Peter Thomson, an Australian graduate student in theology, or the study of religion. Blair has described Thomson as "spellbinding" and "the person who most influenced me."

Thomson introduced him to the works of a Scottish philosopher of the 1930's named John Macmurray, who had a profound impact on the young Blair. Macmurray contended that people were defined by their relationship to the community they lived in, and that a person's self-interest could ultimately benefit the society as a whole.

One result was that Blair firmly committed to the elements of Christian philosophy that pushed for social change. "I had always believed in God," he says, "but I had become slightly detached from it. Peter made it relevant, practical rather than theological. Religion became less of a personal relationship with God. I began to see it in a much more social context."

Blair has been a member of the Labour Party since 1975.

Blair's mother died at the age of 52 from throat cancer.

Even though he hadn't shown much interest in politics during the time that he was in college, he joined the Labour Party in 1975. That was a significant year in his life for two other reasons.

The first was that he graduated from St. John's.

The second happened two weeks later. Blair's mother Hazel died at the age of 52 from throat cancer. Her death deeply affected him. He said, "I suppose you think your mother is indestructible. It never occurs to you that she can die."

Though her death caused him a great deal of pain and anguish, it also made him realize how temporary life is and that if you want to accomplish your goals, you should never procrastinate.

What happened during the next two decades showed that he truly took that lesson to heart. The one-time lead singer for an obscure London rock band soon began a rapid rise to the point where he would become a major world leader.

Chapter 4
From Lawyer to Leader

After graduation, Blair landed a law apprenticeship with the legal firm of Alexander Irvine. At first, Irvine was resistant to the idea because he had already selected another law graduate. However, Blair persuaded Irvine to take him on in addition to the other recruited pupil, Cherie Booth, a top graduate of the London School of Economics.

Little did Tony Blair know that on March 29, 1980, four years after completing his apprenticeship and becoming a lawyer, he would marry Cherie Booth. Amazingly, their courtship withstood their professional rivalry. Only one of them could be given a "tenancy," or permanent position with Irvine. Blair was selected for the tenancy in 1977 even though

Blair landed a law apprenticeship with the legal firm of Alexander Irvine.

Booth had scored much higher on the bar exams. She ended up accepting a tenancy elsewhere.

In an interesting coincidence, Cherie Booth also comes from a show business background. She is the daughter of a famous British actor named Tony Booth, who played the son-in-law in the British TV series *Till Death Us Do Part*. That series provided the original influence for the American sitcom *All in the Family*, which was one of the most popular U.S. shows during the 1980s. Cherie's father played the same role that Rob Reiner portrayed in the U.S. version.

Blair specialized in employment law and took on many

Tony met his wife, Cherie Booth, when they both apprenticed at the same law firm.

important cases which heightened his reputation. Because Alexander Irvine was a prominent member of the Labour Party, Blair met many of its leaders, who talked to him about entering politics.

At that point, the Labour Party was in power. But the Conservative Party took over in 1979. So when Blair made his first attempt to win a seat in Parliament three years after that, he wasn't very successful. Margaret Thatcher was the English prime minister, and she was very popular because she had just led the country to victory in the war with Argentina over the Falkland Islands in the South Atlantic Ocean. Blair came in third and only won 10% of the vote.

But that poor showing didn't discourage him. The very next year, he was elected to Parliament. He won a seat in Sedgefield, a mining district near where he grew up in Durham.

During the next eleven years, Blair rose rapidly in importance in the Labour Party. Finally, in July 1994, he became the party leader. At that time, it had lost four general elections in a row to the Conservatives. So he immediately began to change many of the party's traditional positions so it could appeal to a wider range of voters. His first victory

Tony's employer was a prominent member of the Labour Party. He met many of its leaders, who talked to him about entering politics.

was eliminating a clause in its charter that called for "redistribution of wealth through common ownership of the means of production." Likewise, he placed less emphasis on the party's more traditional goals such as full employment, unilateral nuclear disarmament and the welfare state.

In their place, he advocated free enterprise, making a commitment to fighting inflation, holding down budget deficits, supporting European integration, promising to work for higher education standards to ensure Britain's competitiveness, and more. To show voters that the party had changed, he invented the slogan, "New Labour, New Britain." Within a year, Blair's changes had increased party membership by one-third. The success of his strategy was proven when the party crushed the Conservatives

Tony revitalized the Labour Party with the slogan "New Labour, New Britain."

in nationwide municipal elections in 1995, winning 250 of 258 townships.

The Conservative Party was starting to lose ground. Margaret Thatcher had retired several years earlier and the current leadership wasn't as popular. So it wasn't surprising that the Labour Party captured 419 Parliament seats to the Conservatives' 165 in the 1997 elections in a landslide that went far beyond what most people had expected. As the leader of the new majority party, Blair automatically became the prime minister.

Four months later, Princess Diana was killed in a tragic automobile crash. That became one of the first major tests of Blair's leadership. He endeared himself to his fellow citizens when he hailed Diana as "the people's princess" and strongly encouraged the royal family to confront the grief of the English people head-on.

He also formed close ties with U.S. President Bill Clinton. The two men had many similarities, including their ages, political beliefs and wives who were famous lawyers. While her husband was rapidly rising in politics, Cherie Booth had become a top trial lawyer. Blair always acknowledged that his wife, with a $375,000 salary, was the family breadwinner while he built his political career.

Blair's wife was the family bread–winner while he built his political career.

Chapter 5
Family Life in the Spotlight

After his election, Blair moved his entire family to 10 Downing Street.

Her husband's election as prime minister didn't mean the end of Cherie Booth's working days. She continued her legal practice, wearing her sleek trouser suits as she became the first wife of a British prime minister to have a career outside of the home. But her life became even more hectic as she had to juggle her work assignments and responsibilities for raising children with occasionally accompanying her husband when he traveled on official business.

After his election, Blair moved his entire family to 10 Downing Street, the traditional home of the prime minister. When they moved in, the Blairs had three children: Euan, who was 13 at the time, Nicky, 11, and 9-year-old Kathryn. The Blairs fiercely protect their children's privacy, so not much is known about them.

In spite of his very heavy workload, Tony Blair tries to make his family predominant and minimize disruptions to family life. Michael Beloff, Cherie's former law partner and president of Oxford's Trinity College, said, "The strength they have for the public performance is because they do have a private life that they revere."

The Blair family outside 10 Downing Street.

Whenever possible, the family tries to dine together, and Cherie—despite her own busy schedule—cooks. The family attends church regularly.

But they're not perfect. Euan, the oldest son, was arrested but not charged in July 2000 for drunken behavior following his exams.

"My son is basically a good kid. We will all get through this and see him right," Tony Blair said, even though the episode was embarrassing for him both personally and politically.

Yet his fellow citizens appreciated his openness. It helped him to appear like a real person with the same problems that any family faces.

A much happier event occurred shortly before that. The Blairs added another child, who became the first infant born to a sitting prime minister since 1848.

The English public had been very interested in every aspect of the upcoming birth, and many people even placed bets about what the baby would be named. So there was a lot of excitement when young Leo Blair, who was named after Tony's father, was born on May 20, 2000.

Chapter 6
What the Future
May Hold

No matter how popular a politician may be, there are always people who criticize him or her. That is just as true for Tony Blair as for anyone else.

Some critics accused him of having more style than substance. They agreed that he deserved congratulations for his growing stature as an international statesman. But they added that he may be spreading himself too thin and neglecting the home front. While he was engaged in international diplomacy at a breakneck pace, jetting from London to Oman to Cairo, there were severe domestic issues and problems at home begging for his attention.

Some critics have accused him of having more style than substance.

During his campaign for re-election in June 2001—three months before the terrorist attacks—Blair promised that he would address many of these "home front" issues. He vowed to improve the country's education, health, and transportation systems. He also pledged to work toward securing a lasting peace in Northern Ireland. The voters believed him, because the election results were almost the same as they had been four years earlier. Blair's Labour Party won 413 seats, while the Conservatives won 166.

Despite the country's problems, *The Wash-*

Blair meets with Egyptian President Mohammed Hosni.

ington Post reported after the September 11 attacks that "he presides over the strongest British economy in 40 years." Additionally, *The American Prospect* stated that "Whatever else motivates Tony Blair, then, his post-September 11 stance can also be seen as good domestic politics. He struck the right instinctive note with the public, marginalized his political opponents, and took on his preferred role of strong leader propelled by urgent moral concern."

It is impossible to know how Tony Blair's performance as prime minister will eventually be judged. But one thing is certain: when the United States desperately needed support in the aftermath of the September 11 attacks, Tony Blair proved that he was the best friend that this nation could have had.

Blair has proven that he was the best friend the U.S. could have had.

Chronology

1953   born in Edinburgh, Scotland to Leo Charles Lynton Blair and Hazel Elizabeth Rosaleen Corscaden

late 1950s enters Durham Choristers School in Durham, England

1963   father suffers a stroke and loses ability to speak for three years

1966   enrolls in Fettes College in Edinburgh, Scotland

1971   graduates from Fettes College and takes a year off from school

1972   enters St. John's College at Oxford University and studies law

1975   joins the Labour Party; graduates from St. John's; mother dies

1976   serves as apprentice in law firm of Alexander Irvine, which he later joins as a "tenant"

1980   marries Cherie Booth

1982   loses first election to Parliament

1983   is elected to Parliament

1988   is elected to Labour Party shadow cabinet

1994   wins leadership of the Labour Party after Labour leader John Smith dies

1997   is elected prime minister of Great Britain

2001   is re-elected as prime minister; joins forces with U.S. President George W. Bush to fight war on terrorism

Index

Alexander Irvine 21, 23

Anderson, Eric 15

bin Laden, Osama 7

Blair, Tony (Anthony Charles Lynton)
    birth of 11
    becomes prime minister 25
    children of 26
    early years 11-18
    father suffers stroke 13
    joins Labour Party 20
    joins rock band 17, 18
    marries 21
    mother dies 20
    nicknames 12, 14

    parents of 11
    siblings 11

Blair, Leo (father) 11

Booth, Cherie (wife) 21, 22, 25, 26

Clinton, Bill 10, 25

Corscaden, Hazel (mother) 12

Durham Choristers School 12, 13, 14

Fettes College 14, 17

Labour Party 20, 23

Macmurray, John 18

Milosevic, Slobodan 8, 9, 10

NATO 8, 9, 10

September 11, 2001 5, 31

Thatcher, Margaret 23, 25